Principles of Accounting

SECOND EDITION

Working Papers IA / Chapters 2–14

Principles of Accounting

SECOND EDITION

Working Papers IA / Chapters 2–14

Belverd E. Needles, Jr.
DePaul University
Chicago

Henry R. Anderson
University of
Central Florida

James C. Caldwell
Arthur Andersen & Co.
Dallas/Fort Worth

Houghton Mifflin Company **Boston**
Dallas Geneva, Illinois Hopewell, New Jersey Palo Alto

Printed in the U.S.A.

Library of Congress Catalog Card Number 83-80989

ISBN: 0-395-34333-X

CDEFGHIJ-A-8987654

To the Student

This book contains working papers to be used in preparing solutions to all A Problems in Chapters 2 through 14 of Needles/Anderson/Caldwell, *Principles of Accounting,* Second Edition. The working papers are designed to simplify your work: appropriate forms for each problem are provided, and some preliminary information has been preprinted on them to help you get started. Since there are no problems in Chapter 1, the working papers begin with Chapter 2.

Working Papers

Name

Problem 2A-1
Identification of Transactions

Explanation of each lettered transaction:

a. G. Renfro invested $57,000 cash in a tea company.

b.

c.

d.

e.

f.

g.

h.

Name

Problem 2A-2
Effect of Transactions on Accounting Equation

1 Accounts arranged in equation form   2 Effect of transactions shown

	Assets					=	Liabilities	+ Owner's Equity
	Cash	+	+	+	+ Medical Library	=		+ Helen Knight, Capital
a.	$10,000				$800			$10,800
b.								
Bal.								
c.								
Bal.								
d.								
Bal.								
e.								
Bal.								
f.								
Bal.								
g.								
Bal.								
h.								
Bal.	$	+ $	+ $	+ $	+ $	=	$	+ $

Name

Problem 2A-3
Identification of Transactions

Explanation of transactions on balance sheet:

a. Owner made an investment of $76,000 in a parking lot business.

b.

c.

d.

e.

Name ______________________

Problem 2A-4
Preparation of Financial Statements

Western Riding Club		
Income Statement		
For the Month Ended November 30, 19xx		
Revenues		
Expenses		
Net Income		

Western Riding Club		
Statement of Owner's Equity		
For the Month Ended November 30, 19xx		
Denise Clark, Capital, Nov. 30, 19xx		59000 -

Problem 2A-4 (continued)

Western Riding Club			
Balance Sheet			
November 30, 19xx			
Assets		Liabilities	
		Owner's Equity	
		Denise Clark, Capital	59000 -

Name

Problem 2A-5
Effect of Transactions on Accounting Equation

1 Accounts arranged in equation form *2 Beginning balances entered; capital account computed* *3 Effect of transactions shown*

	Assets									=	Liabilities	+	Owner's Equity
	Cash	+	Accounts Receivable	+	Office Supplies	+	Office Equipment	+	Car	=	Accounts Payable	+	Arthur Moon, Capital
Bal.	$1,900		$680		$300		$1,500		$5,000		$2,600		$
a.													
Bal.													
b.													
Bal.													
c.													
Bal.													
d.													
Bal.													
e.													
Bal.													
f.													
Bal.													
g.													
Bal.													
h.													
Bal.													
i.													
Bal.													
j.													
Bal.													
k.													
Bal.	$	+	$	+	$	+	$	+	$	=	$	+	$

Name

Problem 3A-1
Preparation of Trial Balance

Gibbons Construction Company		
Trial Balance		
April 30, 19xx		
Cash	14920 –	

Name

Problem 3A-2
Transaction Analysis, T Accounts, and Trial Balance

1 T accounts set up

2 Transactions recorded in accounts

Cash

Accounts Receivable

Supplies

Typewriters

Office Equipment

Accounts Payable

Christina Rogers, Capital

Christina Rogers, Withdrawals

Revenue from Business

Rent Expense

Advertising Expense

Salary Expense

Repair Expense

Utility Expense

3 Trial balance completed for current date

Modern Secretary Training Trial Balance (Current Date)		
Cash	6080 -	

Name

Problem 3A-3
Transaction Analysis, T Accounts, and Trial Balance

1 Transactions entered in journal

General Journal

Date		Description	Post. Ref.	Debit	Credit
April	2	Equipment		620 -	
		Cash		4500 -	
		Barry Fisher, Capital			5120
		Invested equipment and cash in business			

Problem 3A-3 (continued)

1 (continued)

General Journal

Date	Description	Post. Ref.	Debit	Credit
April				

Name

Problem 3A-3 (continued)

2 T accounts set up and entries posted from journal

Cash

Accounts Receivable

Supplies

Prepaid Insurance

Equipment

Truck

Accounts Payable

Notes Payable

Barry Fisher, Capital

Barry Fisher, Withdrawals

Painting Fees Earned

Wages Expense

Telephone Expense

Truck Expense

3 Trial balance completed for April 30

Barry Fisher Painting Service Trial Balance April 30, 19xx		
Cash	3670 -	

Name

Problem 3A-4
Using General Journal, T Accounts, and Trial Balance

1 Transactions entered in journal

General Journal					
Date		Description	Post. Ref.	Debit	Credit
Aug.	1	Accounts Payable		220 –	
		Cash			220 –
		Paid for supplies purchased last month			

Problem 3A-4 (continued)

1 (continued)

General Journal				
Date	Description	Post. Ref.	Debit	Credit
Aug.				

Name

Problem 3A-4 (continued)

2 T accounts set up

3 Amounts entered from July 31 trial balance

4 Entries posted from journal

Cash

Accounts Receivable

Supplies

Prepaid Insurance

Equipment

Accounts Payable

Notes Payable

Norm Hopper, Capital

Norm Hopper, Withdrawals

Service Revenue

Rent Expense

Utility Expense

Problem 3A-4 (continued)

5 Trial balance for August 31 completed

Norm's Barber Shop		
Trial Balance		
August 31, 19xx		
	2240	

Name

Problem 3A-5
Relationship of General Journal, Ledger Accounts, and Trial Balances

1 Transactions for February entered in journal

General Journal					Page 17
Date		Description	Post. Ref.	Debit	Credit
Feb.	2	Rent Expense	61	140 -	
		Cash	11		140 -
		Paid one month's rent			

1 *(continued)*

General Journal				Page 18
Date	Description	Post. Ref.	Debit	Credit
Feb.				

Name ______________________

Problem 3A-5 (continued)

2 Ledger accounts set up

3 Amounts from February 1 trial balance entered

4 Entries from journal posted to ledger accounts

General Ledger

Cash — Account No. 11

Date		Item	Post. Ref.	Debit	Credit	Balance Debit	Balance Credit
Feb.	1	Balance				1780 -	

Accounts Receivable — Account No. 12

Date		Item	Post. Ref.	Debit	Credit	Balance Debit	Balance Credit

Supplies — Account No. 13

Date		Item	Post. Ref.	Debit	Credit	Balance Debit	Balance Credit

Prepaid Insurance — Account No. 14

Date		Item	Post. Ref.	Debit	Credit	Balance Debit	Balance Credit

Problem 3A-5 (continued)

2, 3, 4 (continued)

Equipment					Account No. 21	
		Post.			Balance	
Date	Item	Ref.	Debit	Credit	Debit	Credit

Buses					Account No. 22	
		Post.			Balance	
Date	Item	Ref.	Debit	Credit	Debit	Credit

Accounts Payable					Account No. 31	
		Post.			Balance	
Date	Item	Ref.	Debit	Credit	Debit	Credit

Notes Payable					Account No. 32	
		Post.			Balance	
Date	Item	Ref.	Debit	Credit	Debit	Credit

Theresa Tetrault, Capital					Account No. 41	
		Post.			Balance	
Date	Item	Ref.	Debit	Credit	Debit	Credit

Name ______________________________

Problem 3A-5 (continued)

2, 3, 4 (continued)

Theresa Tetrault, Withdrawals — Account No. 42

Date	Item	Post. Ref.	Debit	Credit	Balance Debit	Balance Credit

Service Revenue — Account No. 51

Date	Item	Post. Ref.	Debit	Credit	Balance Debit	Balance Credit

Rent Expense — Account No. 61

Date	Item	Post. Ref.	Debit	Credit	Balance Debit	Balance Credit

Bus Expense — Account No. 62

Date	Item	Post. Ref.	Debit	Credit	Balance Debit	Balance Credit

Wages Expense — Account No. 63

Date	Item	Post. Ref.	Debit	Credit	Balance Debit	Balance Credit

Utility Expense — Account No. 64

Date	Item	Post. Ref.	Debit	Credit	Balance Debit	Balance Credit

Problem 3A-5 (continued)

5 Trial balance for February 29 completed

Daycare Services Company Trial Balance February 29, 19xx		
Cash	1470 –	

Name

Problem 3A-6
Recording and Tracing Transactions from General Journal to Ledger Accounts and Trial Balance

1a Transactions from T accounts entered in journal

General Journal					Page 1
Date		Description	Post. Ref.	Debit	Credit
May	1	Cash	11	2580 -	
		Equipment	21	220 -	
		Mark Kaplan, Capital	41		2800 -
		Invested cash and equipment in business			

Problem 3A-6 (continued)

1b Transactions posted in ledger account form

General Ledger

Cash — Account No. 11

Date		Item	Post. Ref.	Debit	Credit	Balance Debit	Balance Credit
May	1			2580 -		2580 -	

Accounts Receivable — Account No. 12

Date		Item	Post. Ref.	Debit	Credit	Balance Debit	Balance Credit

Supplies — Account No. 13

Date		Item	Post. Ref.	Debit	Credit	Balance Debit	Balance Credit

Prepaid Insurance — Account No. 14

Date		Item	Post. Ref.	Debit	Credit	Balance Debit	Balance Credit

Equipment — Account No. 21

Date		Item	Post. Ref.	Debit	Credit	Balance Debit	Balance Credit
May	1			220 -		220 -	

1b (continued)

Accounts Payable						Account No. 31
					Balance	
Date	Item	Post. Ref.	Debit	Credit	Debit	Credit

Notes Payable						Account No. 32
					Balance	
Date	Item	Post. Ref.	Debit	Credit	Debit	Credit

Mark Kaplan, Capital						Account No. 41
					Balance	
Date	Item	Post. Ref.	Debit	Credit	Debit	Credit
May 1				2800 –		2800 –

Treatment Revenue						Account No. 51
					Balance	
Date	Item	Post. Ref.	Debit	Credit	Debit	Credit

Rent Expense						Account No. 61
					Balance	
Date	Item	Post. Ref.	Debit	Credit	Debit	Credit

Problem 3A-6 (continued)

1c Trial balance completed

Mark Kaplan, Psychiatrist		
Trial Balance		
May 14, 19xx		
Cash	2060 –	

2 By using a general journal and a ledger, Mark Kaplan will have a summary of his business activities because:

a

b

c

Name ______________________

Problem 4A-1
Preparation of Adjusting Entries

General Journal					
Date		Description	Post. Ref.	Debit	Credit
a.					
June	30	Interest Expense			
		Accrued Interest Payable			
		To record accrued interest on mortgage			

Name ______________________

Problem 4A-2
Determining Adjusting Entries from Changes in Trial Balance

General Journal					
Date		Description	Post. Ref.	Debit	Credit
Dec.	31	Accrued Fees Receivable			
		Fees Revenue			
		To record unrecorded fees earned			

Name

Problem 4A-3
Determining Adjusting Entries and Tracing Their Effects to Financial Statements

1 T accounts set up

2 Adjusting entries posted to accounts

Cash

Bal. 742

Accounts Receivable

Prepaid Insurance

Office Supplies

Office Equipment

Accumulated Depreciation, Office Equipment

Copier

Accumulated Depreciation, Copier

Accounts Payable

Unearned Tax Fees

Cynthia Jackson, Capital

Cynthia Jackson, Withdrawals

Fees Revenue

Office Salaries Expense

Advertising Expense

Rent Expense

Telephone Expense

Insurance Expense

Office Supplies Expense

Depreciation Expense, Office Equipment

Depreciation Expense, Copier

3 Adjusted trial balance, income statement, statement of owner's equity, and balance sheet prepared

Jackson Tax Service Adjusted Trial Balance December 31, 19xx		
Cash	742 –	

3 (continued)

Jackson Tax Service		
Income Statement		
For the Year Ended December 31, 19xx		
Revenues		
Expenses		
Net Income		

Jackson Tax Service		
Statement of Owner's Equity		
For the Year Ended Dec. 31, 19xx		

3 (continued)

Jackson Tax Service			
Balance Sheet			
December 31, 19xx			
Assets			
Liabilities			
Owner's Equity			

Name

Problem 4A-4
Determining Adjusting Entries and Tracing Their Effects to Financial Statements

1 T accounts set up

2 Adjusting entries posted to accounts

Cash	
Bal. 1,256	

Accounts Receivable	

Prepaid Insurance	

Cleaning Supplies	

Land	

Building	

Accumulated Depreciation, Building	

Delivery Truck	

Accumulated Depreciation, Delivery Truck	

Accounts Payable	

Wages Payable	

Accrued Interest Payable	

Unearned Dry Cleaning Fees	

Mortgage Payable	

Stanley Lucas, Capital	

Stanley Lucas, Withdrawals	

Dry Cleaning Revenue	

Laundry Revenue	

Plant Wages Expense	

Sales and Delivery Wages Expense	

Cleaning Equipment Rent Expense	

Delivery Truck Expense	

Insurance Expense	

Cleaning Supplies Expense	

Depreciation Expense, Building	

Depreciation Expense, Delivery Truck	

Interest Expense	

Other Expenses	

Problem 4A-4 (continued)

3 Adjusted trial balance prepared

Lucas Dry Cleaning Adjusted Trial Balance September 30, 19xx		
Cash	1256 –	

Name

Problem 4A-4 (continued)

4 Income statement, statement of owner's equity, and balance sheet prepared

Lucas Dry Cleaning Income Statement For the Year Ended September 30, 19xx		
Revenues		
Expenses		
Net Loss		

Lucas Dry Cleaning Statement of Owner's Equity For the Year Ended September 30, 19xx		

4 (continued)

Lucas Dry Cleaning
Balance Sheet
September 30, 19xx

Assets			
Liabilities			
Owner's Equity			

Name

Problem 4A-5
Determining Adjusting Entries and Tracing Their Effects to Financial Statements

2 Adjusting entries recorded in general journal

General Journal

Date		Description	Post. Ref.	Debit	Credit
June	30	Rent Expense	514	6000	
		Prepaid Rent	117		6000
		Paid one year's rent			

1 Ledger accounts opened

3 Adjusting entries posted from the general journal

Cash — Account No. 111

Date		Item	Post. Ref.	Debit	Credit	Balance Debit	Balance Credit

Accounts Receivable — Account No. 112

Date		Item	Post. Ref.	Debit	Credit	Balance Debit	Balance Credit

Prepaid Advertising — Account No. 116

Date		Item	Post. Ref.	Debit	Credit	Balance Debit	Balance Credit

Prepaid Rent — Account No. 117

Date		Item	Post. Ref.	Debit	Credit	Balance Debit	Balance Credit

Prepaid Insurance — Account No. 118

Date		Item	Post. Ref.	Debit	Credit	Balance Debit	Balance Credit

Prepaid Maintenance — Account No. 119

Date		Item	Post. Ref.	Debit	Credit	Balance Debit	Balance Credit

Spare Parts — Account No. 141

Date		Item	Post. Ref.	Debit	Credit	Balance Debit	Balance Credit

Limousines — Account No. 142

Date		Item	Post. Ref.	Debit	Credit	Balance Debit	Balance Credit

Name

Problem 4A-5 (continued)

1, 3 (continued)

Accumulated Depreciation, Limousines — Account No. 143

Date		Item	Post. Ref.	Debit	Credit	Balance Debit	Balance Credit

Notes Payable — Account No. 211

Date		Item	Post. Ref.	Debit	Credit	Balance Debit	Balance Credit

Unearned Passenger Revenue — Account No. 212

Date		Item	Post. Ref.	Debit	Credit	Balance Debit	Balance Credit

Interest Payable — Account No. 213

Date		Item	Post. Ref.	Debit	Credit	Balance Debit	Balance Credit

Norman Sims, Capital — Account No. 311

Date		Item	Post. Ref.	Debit	Credit	Balance Debit	Balance Credit

Norman Sims, Withdrawals — Account No. 312

Date		Item	Post. Ref.	Debit	Credit	Balance Debit	Balance Credit

Passenger Service Revenue — Account No. 411

Date		Item	Post. Ref.	Debit	Credit	Balance Debit	Balance Credit

Gas and Oil Expense — Account No. 511

Date		Item	Post. Ref.	Debit	Credit	Balance Debit	Balance Credit

1, 3 (continued))

Salaries Expense — Account No. 512

Date	Item	Post. Ref.	Debit	Credit	Balance Debit	Balance Credit

Advertising Expense — Account No. 513

Date	Item	Post. Ref.	Debit	Credit	Balance Debit	Balance Credit

Rent Expense — Account No. 514

Date	Item	Post. Ref.	Debit	Credit	Balance Debit	Balance Credit

Insurance Expense — Account No. 515

Date	Item	Post. Ref.	Debit	Credit	Balance Debit	Balance Credit

Spare Parts Expense — Account No. 516

Date	Item	Post. Ref.	Debit	Credit	Balance Debit	Balance Credit

Depreciation Expense, Limousines — Account No. 517

Date	Item	Post. Ref.	Debit	Credit	Balance Debit	Balance Credit

Maintenance Expense — Account No. 518

Date	Item	Post. Ref.	Debit	Credit	Balance Debit	Balance Credit

Interest Expense — Account No. 519

Date	Item	Post. Ref.	Debit	Credit	Balance Debit	Balance Credit

Name ______________________________ **Problem 4A-5 (continued)**

4 Adjusted trial balance, income statement, statement of owner's equity, and balance sheet prepared

Elite Limo Service Adjusted Trial Balance June 30, 19xx		
Cash	10414 –	

4 *(continued)*

Elite Limo Service Income Statement For the Year Ended June 30, 19xx		
Revenues		
Expenses		
Net Income		

Elite Limo Service Statement of Owner's Equity For the Year Ended June 30, 19xx		

Name

Problem 4A-5 (continued)

4 (continued)

Elite Limo Service
Balance Sheet
June 30, 19xx

Assets

Liabilities

Owner's Equity

Name

Problem 4A-6
Correcting Entries and Adjusting Entries and Tracing Their Effects

1 T accounts set up

2 Corrections posted from trial balance for items (a) through (c)

3 Adjusting and correcting entries posted for items (d) through (n)

Metropolitan Answering Service Corrected Trial Balance March 31, 19xx		

Explanation of correcting entries to obtain trial balance:

(a)

(b)

(c)

The new trial balance total is:

Cash	
Bal. 1,907	

Accounts Receivable	

Office Supplies	

Prepaid Insurance	

Prepaid Rent	

Office Equipment	

1, 2, 3 (continued)

Accumulated Depreciation, Office Equipment

Communication Equipment

Accumulated Depreciation, Communication Equipment

Accounts Payable

Wages Payable

Unearned Answering Service Revenue

Lillian Starr, Capital

Lillian Starr, Withdrawals

Answering Service Revenue

Wages Expense

Rent Expense

Office Cleaning Expense

Insurance Expense

Office Supplies Expense

Depreciation Expense, Office Equipment

Depreciation Expense, Communication Equipment

Name ____________________

Problem 4A-6 (continued)

4 Adjusted trial balance, income statement, statement of owner's equity, and balance sheet prepared

Metropolitan Answering Service Adjusted Trial Balance March 31, 19xx		
Cash		

4 (continued)

Metropolitan Answering Service Income Statement For the Three Months Ended March 31, 19xx		
Revenues		
Expenses		
Net Income		

Metropolitan Answering Service Statement of Owner's Equity For the Three Months Ended March 31, 19xx		

Name ______________________

Problem 4A-6 (continued)

4 (continued)

Metropolitan Answering Service Balance Sheet March 31, 19xx			
Assets			
Liabilities			
Owner's Equity			

Name

Problem 5A-1
Completion of Work Sheet

1 Income statement, statement of owner's equity, and balance sheet prepared

Northside Trailer Rental Income Statement For the Year Ended June 30, 19xx		
Revenue		
Expenses		
Net Income		

Northside Trailer Rental Statement of Owner's Equity For the Year Ended June 30, 19xx		

1 (continued)

Northside Trailer Rental

Balance Sheet

June 30, 19xx

Assets

Liabilities

Owner's Equity

Name

Problem 5A-1 (continued)

2 Adjusting, closing, and reversing entries prepared

General Journal

Date		Description	Post. Ref.	Debit	Credit

Name

Problem 5A-2
Preparation of Work Sheet, Adjusting Entries, Closing Entries, and Reversing Entries

1 Work sheet completed (see page 233)

2 Income statement, statement of owner's equity, and balance sheet prepared

James Laughlin, Attorney		
Income Statement		
For the Year Ended December 31, 19xx		
Revenue		
Expenses		
Net Income		

James Laughlin, Attorney		
Statement of Owner's Equity		
For the Year Ended December 31, 19xx		

2 (continued)

James Laughlin, Attorney			
Balance Sheet			
December 31, 19xx			
Assets			
Liabilities			
Owner's Equity			

Name ______________________

Problem 5A-2 (continued)

3 Adjusting, closing, and reversing entries prepared

General Journal				
Date	Description	Post. Ref.	Debit	Credit

4 Comment on results

Name

Problem 5A-3
Completion of Work Sheet, Preparation of Financial Statements, Adjusting Entries, Closing Entries, and Reversing Entries

1 Work sheet completed (see page 235)

2 Income statement, statement of owner's equity, and balance sheet prepared

Drexel Theater Income Statement For the Year Ended September 30, 19xx		
Revenue		
Expenses		
Net Income		

Drexel Theater Statement of Owner's Equity For the Year Ended September 30, 19xx		
Dave Parsons, Capital, Sept. 30, 19xx		171370 –

2 (continued)

Drexel Theater			
Balance Sheet			
September 30, 19xx			
Assets			
Liabilities			
Owner's Equity			

Name

Problem 5A-3 (continued)

3 Adjusting, closing, and reversing entries prepared

General Journal					
Date		Description	Post. Ref.	Debit	Credit

3 (continued)

General Journal				
Date	Description	Post. Ref.	Debit	Credit

Name ______________________

Problem 5A-4
The Complete Accounting Cycle—Two Months

1 Journal entries prepared for May

5 Adjusting and closing entries prepared for May

General Journal — Page 1

Date		Description	Post. Ref.	Debit	Credit

1, 5 (continued)

General Journal — Page 2

Date		Description	Post. Ref.	Debit	Credit

Name

Problem 5A-4 (continued)

2 Accounts opened, May entries posted

5 Adjusting and closing entries posted for May

7 June entries posted

General Ledger

Cash — Account No. 111

Date		Item	Post. Ref.	Debit	Credit	Balance Debit	Balance Credit

Prepaid Insurance — Account No. 117

Date		Item	Post. Ref.	Debit	Credit	Balance Debit	Balance Credit

2, 5, 7 (continued)

Repair Supplies — Account No. 119

Date	Item	Post. Ref.	Debit	Credit	Balance Debit	Balance Credit

Repair Equipment — Account No. 144

Date	Item	Post. Ref.	Debit	Credit	Balance Debit	Balance Credit

Accumulated Depreciation, Repair Equipment — Account No. 145

Date	Item	Post. Ref.	Debit	Credit	Balance Debit	Balance Credit

Accounts Payable — Account No. 212

Date	Item	Post. Ref.	Debit	Credit	Balance Debit	Balance Credit

Mike Peterson, Capital — Account No. 311

Date	Item	Post. Ref.	Debit	Credit	Balance Debit	Balance Credit

2, 5, 7 (continued)

Mike Peterson, Withdrawals — Account No. 312

Date		Item	Post. Ref.	Debit	Credit	Balance Debit	Balance Credit

Income Summary — Account No. 313

Date		Item	Post. Ref.	Debit	Credit	Balance Debit	Balance Credit

Bicycle Repair Revenue — Account No. 411

Date		Item	Post. Ref.	Debit	Credit	Balance Debit	Balance Credit

Store Rent Expense — Account No. 511

Date		Item	Post. Ref.	Debit	Credit	Balance Debit	Balance Credit

2, 5, 7 (continued)

Utility Expense						Account No. 512
		Post.			Balance	
Date	Item	Ref.	Debit	Credit	Debit	Credit

Insurance Expense						Account No. 513
		Post.			Balance	
Date	Item	Ref.	Debit	Credit	Debit	Credit

Repair Supplies Expense						Account No. 514
		Post.			Balance	
Date	Item	Ref.	Debit	Credit	Debit	Credit

Depreciation Expense, Repair Equipment						Account No. 515
		Post.			Balance	
Date	Item	Ref.	Debit	Credit	Debit	Credit

Name

Problem 5A-4 (continued)

7 Journal entries prepared for June

10 Adjusting and closing entries prepared for June

General Journal — Page 3

Date		Description	Post. Ref.	Debit	Credit

7, 10 (continued)

General Journal				Page 4
Date	Description	Post. Ref.	Debit	Credit

Name

Problem 5A-4 (continued)

3 May work sheet completed (see page 237)

4 May income statement, statement of owner's equity, and balance sheet prepared

Peterson Bicycle Repair Store Income Statement For the Month Ended May 31, 19xx		
Revenue		
Expenses		
Net Income		

Peterson Bicycle Repair Store Statement of Owner's Equity For the Month Ended May 31, 19xx		

4 (continued)

Peterson Bicycle Repair Store Balance Sheet May 31, 19xx			
Assets			
Liabilities			
Owner's Equity			

6 May post-closing trial balance prepared

Peterson Bicycle Repair Store Post-Closing Trial Balance May 31, 19xx		
Cash		
Prepaid Insurance		
Repair Supplies		
Repair Equipment		
Accumulated Depreciation, Repair Equipment		
Accounts Payable		
Mike Peterson, Capital		

8 June work sheet completed (see page 239)

9 June income statement, statement of owner's equity, and balance sheet prepared

Peterson Bicycle Repair Store Income Statement For the Month Ended June 30, 19xx		
Revenues		
Expenses		
Net Income		

Peterson Bicycle Repair Store Statement of Owner's Equity For the Month Ended June 30, 19xx		

9 (continued)

Peterson Bicycle Repair Store Balance Sheet June 30, 19xx			
Assets			
Liabilities			
Owner's Equity			

11 June post-closing trial balance prepared

Peterson Bicycle Repair Store Post-Closing Trial Balance June 30, 19xx		
Cash		
Prepaid Insurance		
Repair Supplies		
Repair Equipment		
Accumulated Depreciation, Repair Equipment		
Accounts Payable		
Mike Peterson, Capital		

Name

Problem 5A-5
Preparation of Work Sheet from Limited Data

1 Work sheet completed (see page 241)

2 Adjusting entries and explanations prepared

General Journal				
Date	Description	Post. Ref.	Debit	Credit

3 Statement of owner's equity and balance sheet prepared

Eastmoor Bowling Lanes Statement of Owner's Equity For the Year Ended December 31, 19xx		

3 (continued)

Eastmoor Bowling Lanes Balance Sheet December 31, 19xx		
Assets		
Liabilities		
Owner's Equity		

Name

Problem 6A-1
Merchandising Transactions

1 Purchases recorded initially at gross purchase price

General Journal

Date		Description	Post. Ref.	Debit	Credit

1 (continued)

General Journal

Date	Description	Post. Ref.	Debit	Credit

Name Problem 6A-1 (continued)

2 Changes required for net purchases method described:

Name

Problem 6A-2
Work Sheet, Income Statement, Balance Sheet, and Closing Entries for Merchandising Concern

1a, b Work sheets completed—adjusting entry and closing entry methods (see pages 243–245)

2 Income statement and balance sheet prepared

Pepitone Book Store			
Income Statement			
For the Period Ended June 30, 19x2			
Revenue from Sales			

2 (continued)

Pepitone Bookstore			
Balance Sheet			
June 30, 19x2			
Assets			
Liabilities			
Owner's Equity			

3a Closing entries prepared—adjusting entry method

General Journal

Date		Description	Post. Ref.	Debit	Credit

Problem 6A-2 (continued)

3b Closing entries prepared—closing entry method

General Journal

Date	Description	Post. Ref.	Debit	Credit

Name

Problem 6A-3
Journalizing Transactions of a Merchandising Company

Transactions recorded using gross method of recording purchases

General Journal

Date		Description	Post. Ref.	Debit	Credit

Problem 6A-3 (continued)

General Journal				
Date	Description	Post. Ref.	Debit	Credit

Name

Problem 6A-3 (continued)

General Journal				
Date	Description	Post. Ref.	Debit	Credit

Changes required if the net method of recording purchases were used

Name

Problem 6A-4
Work Sheet, Income Statement, and Closing Entries for Merchandising Concern

1a, b Work sheets prepared—adjusting entry and closing entry methods *(see pages 247–249)*

2. Income statement prepared

McCandlish's Shoe Store

Income Statement

For the Year Ended December 31, 19xx

Revenue from Sales			

3a Closing entries prepared—adjusting entry method

General Journal				
Date	Description	Post. Ref.	Debit	Credit

Name ____________________

Problem 6A-4 (continued)

3b Closing entries prepared—closing entry method

General Journal

Date		Description	Post. Ref.	Debit	Credit

Name

Problem 6A-5
Work Sheet, Income Statement, and Closing Entries for Merchandising Concern

1a, b Work sheets completed—adjusting entry and closing entry methods (see pages 251–253)

2 Income statement prepared

Barney's Camera Store			
Income Statement			
For the Year Ended June 30, 19xx			
Revenue from Sales			

3a Closing entries prepared—adjusting entry method

General Journal

Date	Description	Post. Ref.	Debit	Credit

Name ______________________

Problem 6A-5 (continued)

3b Closing entries prepared—closing entry method

General Journal

Date		Description	Post. Ref.	Debit	Credit

3b (continued)

General Journal

Date	Description	Post. Ref.	Debit	Credit

Name ______________________

Problem 7A-1
Identification of Transactions

1 Sales transactions identified

May 31

May 31

May 31

2 Accounts receivable transactions identified

May 5

May 9

May 15

Name ______________________________

Problem 7A-2
Cash Receipts and Cash Payments Journals

1 Transactions entered in cash receipts and cash payments journals

2 Journals footed and ruled

Cash Receipts Journal

Date	Account Credited	Post. Ref.	Credits			Debits	
			Other Accounts	Accounts Receivable	Sales	Sales Discounts	Cash

1, 2 (continued)

Cash Payments Journal

					Debits		Credits	
Date	Ck. No.	Payee	Other Account Debited	Post. Ref.	Other Accounts	Accounts Payable	Purchases Discounts	Cash

Name

Problem 7A-3
Purchases and General Journals

1 Transactions entered in general journal and purchases journal

General Journal				Page 1
Date	Description	Post. Ref.	Debit	Credit

1 (continued) *2 Purchases journal footed and ruled*

Purchases Journal									Page 1
					Credit	Debits			
		Date of		Post.	Accounts		Freight	Store	Office
Date	Account Credited	Invoice	Terms	Ref.	Payable	Purchases	In	Supplies	Supplies

Name

Problem 7A-3 (continued)

3 General ledger and accounts payable subsidiary ledger accounts opened and amounts posted

General Ledger

Store Supplies — Account No. 116

Date		Item	Post. Ref.	Debit	Credit	Balance Debit	Balance Credit

Office Supplies — Account No. 117

Date		Item	Post. Ref.	Debit	Credit	Balance Debit	Balance Credit

Lawn Equipment — Account No. 142

Date		Item	Post. Ref.	Debit	Credit	Balance Debit	Balance Credit

Display Equipment — Account No. 144

Date		Item	Post. Ref.	Debit	Credit	Balance Debit	Balance Credit

Cleaning Equipment — Account No. 146

Date		Item	Post. Ref.	Debit	Credit	Balance Debit	Balance Credit

Accounts Payable — Account No. 211

Date		Item	Post. Ref.	Debit	Credit	Balance Debit	Balance Credit

Problem 7A-3 (continued)

3 (continued)

Purchases					Account No. 611	
		Post.			Balance	
Date	Item	Ref.	Debit	Credit	Debit	Credit

Freight In					Account No. 612	
		Post.			Balance	
Date	Item	Ref.	Debit	Credit	Debit	Credit

Accounts Payable Ledger

Bogart Supply, Inc.					
Date	Item	Post. Ref.	Debit	Credit	Balance

E-Z Lawn Equipment Company					
Date	Item	Post. Ref.	Debit	Credit	Balance

Horne Fertilizer Company					
Date	Item	Post. Ref.	Debit	Credit	Balance

Target Company					
Date	Item	Post. Ref.	Debit	Credit	Balance

Name

Problem 7A-4
Comprehensive Use of Special-Purpose Journals

1 Special-purpose and general journals prepared

5 Transactions entered

6 Journals footed

Sales Journal				Page 1
Date	Account Debited	Invoice Number	Post. Ref.	Amount

Purchases Journal					Page 1
Date	Account Credited	Date of Invoice	Terms	Post. Ref.	Amount

Cash Receipts Journal							Page 1
			Credits			Debits	
Date	Account Credited	Post. Ref.	Other Accounts	Accounts Receivable	Sales	Sales Discounts	Cash

1, 5, 6 (continued)

Cash Payments Journal								Page 1
					Debits		Credits	
	Ck.		Other	Post.	Other	Accounts	Purchases	
Date	No.	Payee	Account Debited	Ref.	Accounts	Payable	Discounts	Cash

1, 5 (continued)

General Journal				Page 1
Date	Description	Post. Ref.	Debit	Credit

2 General ledger accounts opened and transactions posted

General Ledger

Cash — Account No. 111

Date		Item	Post. Ref.	Debit	Credit	Balance Debit	Balance Credit

Accounts Receivable — Account No. 112

Date		Item	Post. Ref.	Debit	Credit	Balance Debit	Balance Credit

Prepaid Insurance — Account No. 113

Date		Item	Post. Ref.	Debit	Credit	Balance Debit	Balance Credit

Accounts Payable — Account No. 211

Date		Item	Post. Ref.	Debit	Credit	Balance Debit	Balance Credit

Name

Problem 7A-4 (continued)

2 (continued)

Sales						Account No. 411
		Post.			Balance	
Date	Item	Ref.	Debit	Credit	Debit	Credit

Sales Discounts						Account No. 412
		Post.			Balance	
Date	Item	Ref.	Debit	Credit	Debit	Credit

Sales Returns and Allowances						Account No. 413
		Post.			Balance	
Date	Item	Ref.	Debit	Credit	Debit	Credit

Purchases						Account No. 511
		Post.			Balance	
Date	Item	Ref.	Debit	Credit	Debit	Credit

Purchases Discounts						Account No. 512
		Post.			Balance	
Date	Item	Ref.	Debit	Credit	Debit	Credit

Purchases Returns and Allowances						Account No. 513
		Post.			Balance	
Date	Item	Ref.	Debit	Credit	Debit	Credit

Problem 7A-4 (continued)

2 (continued)

Freight In					Account No. 514	
		Post.			Balance	
Date	Item	Ref.	Debit	Credit	Debit	Credit

Salaries Expense					Account No. 521	
		Post.			Balance	
Date	Item	Ref.	Debit	Credit	Debit	Credit

Advertising Expense					Account No. 522	
		Post.			Balance	
Date	Item	Ref.	Debit	Credit	Debit	Credit

Rent Expense					Account No. 531	
		Post.			Balance	
Date	Item	Ref.	Debit	Credit	Debit	Credit

Utilities Expense					Account No. 532	
		Post.			Balance	
Date	Item	Ref.	Debit	Credit	Debit	Credit

Name ______________________ **Problem 7A-4 (continued)**

3 Accounts receivable subsidiary ledger accounts opened and transactions posted

Accounts Receivable Subsidiary Ledger

C. Daniels

Date		Item	Post. Ref.	Debit	Credit	Balance

R. McCray

Date		Item	Post. Ref.	Debit	Credit	Balance

T. Schultz

Date		Item	Post. Ref.	Debit	Credit	Balance

4 Accounts payable subsidiary ledger accounts opened and transactions posted

Accounts Payable Subsidiary Ledger

Jayson, Inc.

Date		Item	Post. Ref.	Debit	Credit	Balance

Landon Transit

Date		Item	Post. Ref.	Debit	Credit	Balance

Perkins Company

Date		Item	Post. Ref.	Debit	Credit	Balance

WRBB

Date		Item	Post. Ref.	Debit	Credit	Balance

7 Trial balance and schedules of accounts receivable and accounts payable prepared

Alamo Office Supply Company
Trial Balance
November 30, 19xx

Alamo Office Supply Company
Schedule of Accounts Receivable
November 30, 19xx

Alamo Office Supply Company
Schedule of Accounts Payable
November 30, 19xx

Name

Problem 7A-5
Comprehensive Use of Special Purpose Journals

1 Special-purpose journals prepared
5 Transactions entered
6 Journals footed

Sales Journal				Page 1
Date	Account Debited	Invoice Number	Post. Ref.	Amount

Purchases Journal					Page 1
Date	Account Credited	Date of Invoice	Terms	Post. Ref.	Amount

Cash Receipts Journal							Page 1
			Credits			Debits	
Date	Account Credited	Post. Ref.	Other Accounts	Accounts Receivable	Sales	Sales Discounts	Cash

1, 5, 6 (continued)

Cash Payments Journal

Page 1

Date	Ck. No.	Payee	Other Account Debited	Post. Ref.	Debits: Other Accounts	Debits: Accounts Payable	Credits: Purchases Discounts	Credits: Cash

1, 5 (continued)

General Journal

Date	Description	Post. Ref.	Debit	Credit

2 General ledger accounts opened and transactions posted

General Ledger

Cash						Account No. 111
		Post.			Balance	
Date	Item	Ref.	Debit	Credit	Debit	Credit

Accounts Receivable						Account No. 112
		Post.			Balance	
Date	Item	Ref.	Debit	Credit	Debit	Credit

Store Equipment						Account No. 141
		Post.			Balance	
Date	Item	Ref.	Debit	Credit	Debit	Credit

Accounts Payable						Account No. 211
		Post.			Balance	
Date	Item	Ref.	Debit	Credit	Debit	Credit

Name

Problem 7A-5 (continued)

2 (continued)

Notes Payable — Account No. 212

Date		Item	Post. Ref.	Debit	Credit	Balance Debit	Balance Credit

Wendell Jordon, Capital — Account No. 311

Date		Item	Post. Ref.	Debit	Credit	Balance Debit	Balance Credit

Sales — Account No. 411

Date		Item	Post. Ref.	Debit	Credit	Balance Debit	Balance Credit

Sales Discounts — Account No. 412

Date		Item	Post. Ref.	Debit	Credit	Balance Debit	Balance Credit

Sales Returns and Allowances — Account No. 413

Date		Item	Post. Ref.	Debit	Credit	Balance Debit	Balance Credit

Purchases — Account No. 511

Date		Item	Post. Ref.	Debit	Credit	Balance Debit	Balance Credit

2 (continued)

Purchases Discounts — Account No. 512

Date	Item	Post. Ref.	Debit	Credit	Balance Debit	Balance Credit

Purchases Returns and Allowances — Account No. 513

Date	Item	Post. Ref.	Debit	Credit	Balance Debit	Balance Credit

Freight In — Account No. 514

Date	Item	Post. Ref.	Debit	Credit	Balance Debit	Balance Credit

Sales Salaries Expense — Account No. 611

Date	Item	Post. Ref.	Debit	Credit	Balance Debit	Balance Credit

Advertising Expense — Account No. 612

Date	Item	Post. Ref.	Debit	Credit	Balance Debit	Balance Credit

Rent Expense — Account No. 613

Date	Item	Post. Ref.	Debit	Credit	Balance Debit	Balance Credit

Name ______________________________

Problem 7A-5 (continued)

3 Accounts receivable subsidiary ledger accounts opened and transactions posted

Accounts Receivable Subsidiary Ledger

Roy Fields

Date		Item	Post. Ref.	Debit	Credit	Balance

Meg Taylor

Date		Item	Post. Ref.	Debit	Credit	Balance

University Center

Date		Item	Post. Ref.	Debit	Credit	Balance

4 Accounts payable subsidiary ledger accounts opened and transactions posted

Accounts Payable Subsidiary Ledger

Diamond Books, Inc.

Date		Item	Post. Ref.	Debit	Credit	Balance

Gateway Books

Date		Item	Post. Ref.	Debit	Credit	Balance

Parcel Shippers

Date		Item	Post. Ref.	Debit	Credit	Balance

Victory Publishing Company

Date		Item	Post. Ref.	Debit	Credit	Balance

Name ______________________

7 Trial balance, schedules of accounts receivable and payable prepared

Jordon Book Store
Trial Balance
September 30, 19xx

Jordon Book Store
Schedule of Accounts Receivable
September 30, 19xx

Jordon Book Store
Schedule of Accounts Payable
September 30, 19xx

Name ______________________

Problem 8A-1
Petty Cash Transactions

General Journal				
Date	Description	Post. Ref.	Debit	Credit

Name

Problem 8A-2
Bank Reconciliation

1 Bank reconciliation prepared

Mike Grove Company Bank Reconciliation October 31, 19xx		

2 Adjusting entries prepared

General Journal				
Date	Description	Post. Ref.	Debit	Credit

3

Name ______________________

Problem 8A-3
Bank Reconciliation

1 Bank reconciliation prepared

Bexley Company
Bank Reconciliation
February 28, 19xx

Problem 8A-3 (continued)

2 Adjusting entries prepared

General Journal				
Date	Description	Post. Ref.	Debit	Credit

3 Cash balance on February 28:

Name

Problem 8A-4
Internal Control

1 Weakness in internal control system identified

2 Improvements suggested

Name

Problem 8A-5
Voucher System Transactions

1 Voucher register, check register, and journal entries prepared and transactions recorded *(see page 255 for voucher register)*

Check Register

Ck. No.	Date	Payee	Vou. No.	Debit Vouchers Payable	Credits Purchases Discounts	Credits Cash

General Journal

Date	Description	Post. Ref.	Debit	Credit

Problem 8A-5 (continued)

2 Vouchers Payable account prepared, and entries posted

Vouchers Payable						Account No. 211
					Balance	
Date	Item	Post. Ref.	Debit	Credit	Debit	Credit

3 Schedule of unpaid vouchers prepared

F and R Company Schedule of Unpaid Vouchers January 31, 19xx		
Payee	Voucher No.	Amount

Name ______________________

Problem 8A-6
Voucher System Transactions

1 Voucher register, check register, and journal entries prepared *(see page 257 for voucher register)*

Check Register

Ck. No.	Date	Payee	Vou. No.	Debit: Vouchers Payable	Credits: Purchases Discounts	Credits: Cash

General Journal

Date	Description	Post. Ref.	Debit	Credit

Problem 8A-6 (continued)

2 Vouchers Payable account prepared, and entries posted

Vouchers Payable						Account No. 211
		Post.			Balance	
Date	Item	Ref.	Debit	Credit	Debit	Credit

3 Schedule of unpaid vouchers prepared

Afshar Fashions Schedule of Unpaid Vouchers May 31, 19xx		
Payee	Voucher No.	Amount

Name

Problem 9A-1
Accounting Conventions

1 Convention:
Explanation:
2 Convention:
Explanation:
3 Convention:
Explanation:
4 Convention:
Explanation:
5 Convention:
Explanation:

Name

Problem 9A-2
Forms of the Income Statement

1 Income statement prepared

Sher Hardware Company
Income Statement
For the Year Ended June 30, 19x2

2 Condensed income statement in multistep form prepared

Sher Hardware Company

Income Statement

For the Year Ended June 30, 19x2

3 Condensed income statement in single-step form prepared

Sher Hardware Company

Income Statement

For the Year Ended June 30, 19x2

Name

Problem 9A-3
Classified Balance Sheet

Sher Hardware Company
Balance Sheet
June 30, 19xx

Name

Problem 9A-4
Ratio Analysis—Liquidity and Profitability

1 Liquidity measures computed

a Working capital

b Current ratio

Comment:

2 Profitability measures computed

a Profit margin

b Return on assets

c Debt to equity

d Return on equity

Comment:

Name ____________________

Problem 9A-5

Multistep Income Statement

1 Condensed multistep income statement prepared

Judy's Candy Shop

Income Statement

For the Year Ended December 31, 19xx

Problem 9A-5 (continued)

2 Errors on Linda's income statement:

3 Advantages of using multistep income statement:

Name

Problem 9A-6
Classified Financial Statement Preparation and Evaluation

1a Multistep income statement prepared

Sunshine Lawn Equipment Center
Income Statement
For the Year Ended December 31, 19xx

1b Statement of owner's equity prepared

Sunshine Lawn Equipment Center
Statement of Owner's Equity
For the Year Ended December 31, 19xx

1c Classified balance sheet prepared

Sunshine Lawn Equipment Center
Balance Sheet
December 31, 19xx

2 Liquidity measures computed

a Working capital

b Current ratio

3 Profitability measures computed

a Profit margin

b Return on assets

c Debt to equity

d Return on equity

Name

Problem 9A-7
Classified Financial Statement Preparation and Evaluation

1a Single-step income statement prepared

Carlton Corporation
Income Statement
For the Year Ended December 31, 19xx

Problem 9A-7 (continued)

1b Classified balance sheet prepared

Carlton Corporation Balance Sheet December 31, 19xx			

Name

Problem 9A-7 (continued)

1b Classified balance sheet prepared (continued)

Carlton Corporation

Balance Sheet

December 31, 19xx

Problem 9A-7 (continued)

2a Liquidity measures computed

Working capital

Current ratio

2b Profitability measures computed

Profit margin

Return on assets

Debt to equity

Return on equity

Name

Problem 10A-1
Percentage of Net Sales Method

1 Summary journal entries prepared

2 Entry for estimated uncollectible accounts expense prepared

General Journal

Date	Description	Post. Ref.	Debit	Credit

3 Ledger accounts opened, beginning balances entered, and transactions posted

General Ledger

Accounts Receivable — Account No. 112

Date	Item	Post. Ref.	Debit	Credit	Balance Debit	Balance Credit

Allowance for Uncollectible Accounts — Account No. 113

Date	Item	Post. Ref.	Debit	Credit	Balance Debit	Balance Credit

Name

Problem 10A-2
Accounts Receivable Aging Method

1 Aging analysis of accounts receivable completed

Vander Molen Department Store
Aging Analysis of Accounts Receivable
January 31, 19xx

Customer Account	Total	Not Yet Due	1–30 Days Past Due	31–60 Days Past Due	61–90 Days Past Due	Over 90 Days Past Due
Balance forward	66470 0 –	35456 0 –	14460 0 –	8540 0 –	4640 0 –	3374 0 –

2 End-of-year balance computed

3 Analysis of uncollectible accounts prepared

Vander Molen Department Store			
Estimated Uncollectible Accounts			
January 31, 19xx			
	Amount	Percentage Considered Uncollectible	Allowance for Uncollectible Accounts

4 Journal entry for uncollectible accounts prepared

General Journal				
Date	Description	Post. Ref.	Debit	Credit

Name ______________________

Problem 10A-3
Notes Receivable Transactions

General Journal

Date	Description	Post. Ref.	Debit	Credit

General Journal

Date		Description	Post. Ref.	Debit	Credit

Name ______________________________

Problem 10A-4
Notes Receivable Transactions

General Journal

Date		Description	Post. Ref.	Debit	Credit

Problem 10A-4 (continued)

General Journal				
Date	Description	Post. Ref.	Debit	Credit

Name

Problem 10A-5
Short-Term Financing by Discounting Customers' Notes

1 Journal entries for September prepared

General Journal

Date	Description	Post. Ref.	Debit	Credit

Problem 10A-5 (continued)

2 Cash generated during September computed

3 Journal entries for January prepared

General Journal					
Date		Description	Post. Ref.	Debit	Credit

4 Plan evaluated, etc.

Name

Problem 11A-1
Inventory Cost Methods

1 Schedule prepared

Zack Company Schedule of Cost of Goods Available for Sale During 19xx	Units	Price	Total Cost
Beginning Inventory			
Purchases			

2a Income statement prepared—average cost basis

Zack Company Income Statement For the Year Ended December 31, 19xx			

Problem 11A-1 (continued)

2b Income statement prepared—FIFO basis

Zack Company

Income Statement

For the Year Ended December 31, 19xx

2c Income statement prepared—LIFO basis

Zack Company

Income Statement

For the Year Ended December 31, 19xx

Name ______________________

Problem 11A-2
Lower-of-Cost-or-Market Method

1 Inventory value computed, using item-by-item method

Inventory Type or Item	Quantity	Per Unit Cost	Per Unit Market			Lower of Cost or Market
Product line 1						
Item 11	340	10 00	10 00			
Item 12	540	8 00	10 00			
Item 13	420	16 00	14 00			
Product line 2						
Item 21	220	30 00	34 00			
Item 22	800	42 00	40 00			
Item 23	140	36 00	40 00			
Product line 3						
Item 31	740	52 00	40 00			
Item 32	620	60 00	56 00			
Item 33	240	68 00	78 00			

2 Inventory value computed, using major category method

Inventory Type or Item	Quantity	Per Unit Cost	Per Unit Market	Total Cost	Total Market	Lower of Cost or Market
Product line 1						
Item 11	340	10 00	10 00			
Item 12	540	8 00	10 00			
Item 13	420	16 00	14 00			
Product line 2						
Item 21	220	30 00	34 00			
Item 22	800	42 00	40 00			
Item 23	140	36 00	40 00			
Product line 3						
Item 31	740	52 00	40 00			
Item 32	620	60 00	56 00			
Item 33	240	68 00	78 00			

Name ______________________

Problem 11A-3
Perpetual Inventory System

1 Perpetual inventory card prepared—FIFO basis

Item: Product Z54

Date	Received			Sold			Balance		
	Units	Cost	Total	Units	Cost	Total	Units	Cost	Balance

Problem 11A-3 (continued)

2 Perpetual inventory card prepared—LIFO basis

Item: Product Z54

Date	Received			Sold			Balance		
	Units	Cost	Total	Units	Cost	Total	Units	Cost	Balance

3, 4 Journal entries prepared

General Journal					
Date		Description	Post. Ref.	Debit	Credit

Name

Problem 11A-4
Periodic Inventory System

1 Value of ending inventory computed under periodic system—FIFO basis

	Units	Unit Price	Amount

2 Value of ending inventory computed under periodic system—LIFO basis

	Units	Unit Price	Amount

3 Journal entry prepared

General Journal

Date	Description	Post. Ref.	Debit	Credit

Name

Problem 11A-5
Retail Inventory Method

1, 2, 3 Schedule prepared

	Cost	Retail

Name ______________________

Problem 11A-6

Gross Profit Method

Mueller Bros.

Schedule of Estimated Inventory Loss

May 22, 19xx

Name

Problem 12A-1
Payroll Entries

1, 2, 3, 4 Journal entries prepared

General Journal				
Date	Description	Post. Ref.	Debit	Credit

Name ______________________

Problem 12A-2

Product Warranty Liability

1a, b Journal entries prepared

General Journal				
Date	Description	Post. Ref.	Debit	Credit

2 Balance of estimated product warranty liabilities computed

Name

Problem 12A-3

Notes Payable Transactions and End-of-Period Entries

1 Journal entries prepared

General Journal

Date	Description	Post. Ref.	Debit	Credit

2 Accounts opened and amounts posted

General Ledger

Notes Payable — Account No. 212

Date		Item	Post. Ref.	Debit	Credit	Balance Debit	Balance Credit

Discount on Notes Payable — Account No. 213

Date		Item	Post. Ref.	Debit	Credit	Balance Debit	Balance Credit

Interest Payable — Account No. 214

Date		Item	Post. Ref.	Debit	Credit	Balance Debit	Balance Credit

Interest Expense — Account No. 721

Date		Item	Post. Ref.	Debit	Credit	Balance Debit	Balance Credit

Name ______________________

Problem 12A-4
Property Tax and Vacation Pay Liabilities

1 Monthly tax computed and journal entries prepared

General Journal

Date	Description	Post. Ref.	Debit	Credit

2a Vacation pay computed

2b, c Journal entries prepared

General Journal

Date	Description	Post. Ref.	Debit	Credit

Name

Problem 12A-5
FICA and Unemployment Taxes

1 Schedule of employee earnings prepared

South Haven Company Schedule of Wages Subject to Payroll Taxes			
Employee Name	Cumulative Earnings	Subject to FICA	Subject to Unemployment Taxes
Axmear, J.	14850 -		
Bado, R.	2936 -		
Damte, N.	3239 -		
Edens, T.	9470 -		
Huden, P.	38200 -		
Lupe, D.	15900 -		
Lu, C.	6900 -		
Nelson, K.	10211 -		
Trezzo, J.	3140 -		
Voss, B.	13650 -		
Votaw, A.	9871 -		
Walker, H.	8392 -		

2 FICA and unemployment taxes computed

Name

Problem 12A-6
Payroll Register and Related Entries

1 Payroll register prepared (see page 259)

2, 3 Journal entries prepared

General Journal

Date		Description	Post. Ref.	Debit	Credit

Name

Problem 13A-1
Comparison of Depreciation Methods

1 Annual depreciation computed

End of Year	Straight-Line Carrying Value	Straight-Line Depreciation	Sum-of-the-Years'-Digits Carrying Value	Sum-of-the-Years'-Digits Depreciation	Declining-Balance Carrying Value	Declining-Balance Depreciation*
Date of Purchase						
1						
2						
3						
4						
5						
6						

*Rounded to nearest dollar

2 Graphs for depreciation and carrying value prepared

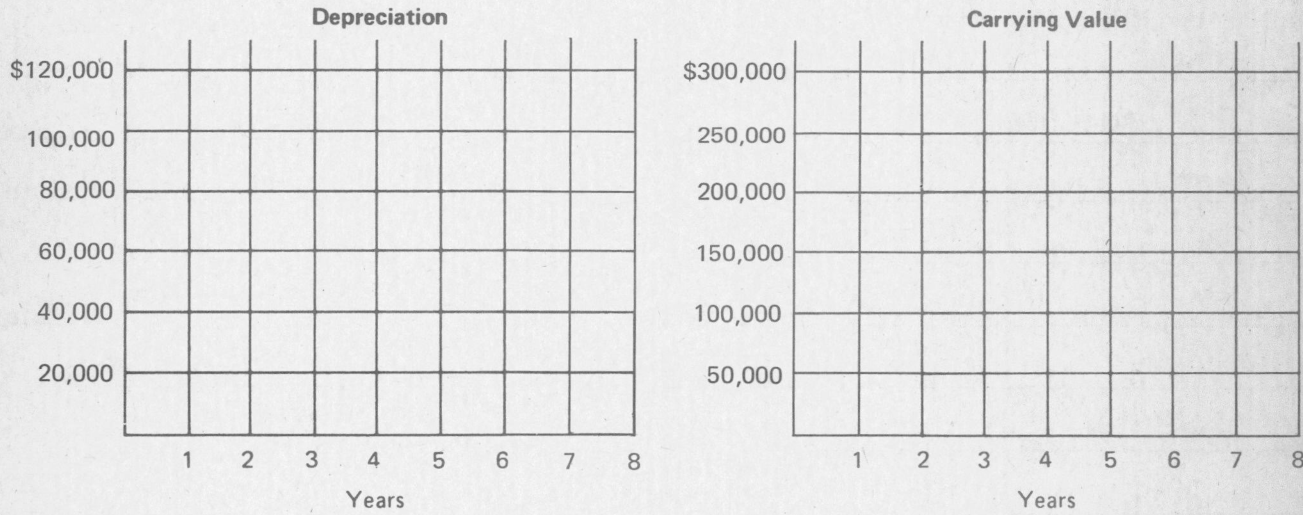

3 Conclusions drawn from graphs

Name

Problem 13A-2
Determining Cost of Plant Assets

1 Schedule prepared

Doda Company
Schedule of Proper Charges to Asset and Loss Accounts
December 31, 19xx

	Land	Land Improvements	Buildings	Machinery	Losses

2, 3 Adjusting entries prepared

General Journal				
Date	Description	Post. Ref.	Debit	Credit

Name

Problem 13A-3

Depreciation Methods and Partial Years

Depreciation Table				
Equip. No.	Computations	Depreciation		
		19x1	19x2	19x3

Name ______________________________

Problem 13A-4
Plant Asset Transactions, Revised Depreciation, and Spare Parts

1 Journal entries prepared for 19x1

General Journal				
Date	Description	Post. Ref.	Debit	Credit

2 Journal entries prepared for 19x2

General Journal

Date	Description	Post. Ref.	Debit	Credit

Name

Problem 13A-5

Plant Asset Transactions and Record Cards

1 Journal entries prepared

General Journal

Date		Description	Post. Ref.	Debit	Credit

Problem 13A-5 (continued)

1 (continued)

General Journal				
Date	Description	Post. Ref.	Debit	Credit

3 Schedule prepared

Ms. Wares Bread Company Schedule of Delivery Equipment Balance December 31, 19x3		
Plant Asset No.	Delivery Equipment	Accumulated Depreciation

Name

Problem 13A-5 (continued)

2 Ledger accounts opened, plant asset record cards prepared, and amounts from journal posted

General Ledger

Delivery Equipment — Account No. 143

Date	Item	Post. Ref.	Debit	Credit	Balance Debit	Balance Credit

Accumulated Depreciation, Delivery Equipment — Account No. 144

Date	Item	Post. Ref.	Debit	Credit	Balance Debit	Balance Credit

Subsidiary Plant Asset and Depreciation Record — **Plant Asset No.:**

Item: — **Serial No.:**

General Ledger Account:

Purchased from:

Where Located:

Person Responsible for Asset:

Estimated Life: — **Estimated Residual Value:**

Depreciation Method: — **Depreciation per Year:** — **Mo.:**

Date	Explanation	Post. Ref.	Asset Record Dr.	Asset Record Cr.	Asset Record Bal.	Depreciation Dr.	Depreciation Cr.	Depreciation Bal.

2 (continued)

Subsidiary Plant Asset and Depreciation Record — Plant Asset No.:

Item: — Serial No.:
General Ledger Account:
Purchased from:
Where Located:
Person Responsible for Asset:
Estimated Life: — Estimated Residual Value:
Depreciation Method: — Depreciation per Year: — Mo.:

Date	Explanation	Post. Ref.	Asset Record Dr.	Asset Record Cr.	Asset Record Bal.	Depreciation Dr.	Depreciation Cr.	Depreciation Bal.

Subsidiary Plant Asset and Depreciation Record — Plant Asset No.:

Item: — Serial No.:
General Ledger Account:
Purchased from:
Where Located:
Person Responsible for Asset:
Estimated Life: — Estimated Residual Value:
Depreciation Method: — Depreciation per Year: — Mo.:

Date	Explanation	Post. Ref.	Asset Record Dr.	Asset Record Cr.	Asset Record Bal.	Depreciation Dr.	Depreciation Cr.	Depreciation Bal.

Name

Problem 13A-6
Comprehensive Problem: Initial Recording, Depreciation Methods, and Disposals

Journal entries prepared

General Journal

Date	Description	Post. Ref.	Debit	Credit

Problem 13A-6 (continued)

General Journal				
Date	Description	Post. Ref.	Debit	Credit

Name

Problem 13A-7
Comprehensive Natural Resource Entries

1, 2 Journal entries prepared

General Journal				
Date	Description	Post. Ref.	Debit	Credit

3 Income statement prepared

Daniels Gravel Company
Income Statement
For the Year Ended December 31, 19x2

Name ______________________________

Problem 14A-1
Effect of Alternative Accounting Methods

1 Alternative income statements prepared

Hilliard Company		
Alternative Income Statements		
For the Year Ended December 31, 19xx		
Income Statement Using FIFO and Straight-Line		
Income Statement Using LIFO and Sum-of-the-Years'-Digits		

Problem 14A-1 (continued)

2 Schedule prepared

Hilliard Company

Schedule of Differences in Net Income

For the Year Ended December 31, 19xx

Name

Problem 14A-2
Amortization of Exclusive License

General Journal

Date		Description	Post. Ref.	Debit	Credit

Name

Problem 14A-3
Amortization of Leasehold and Leasehold Improvements

General Journal				
Date	Description	Post. Ref.	Debit	Credit

Name ______________________

Problem 14A-4

Calculation of Purchasing Power Gain or Loss and Balance Sheet Restatement

1 Purchasing power gain or loss calculated

	Recorded Amount	Conversion Factor	Restated Amount	Gain or (Loss)

Problem 14A-4 (continued)

2 Balance sheet restated

Eastmoor Skating, Inc. Restatement of Balance Sheet December 31, 19x2			
	Recorded Amount	Conversion Factor	Restated Amount

Name

Problem 14A-5

Comprehensive Capital and Revenue Expenditure Entries

1 Journal entries prepared for 1970–1980 transactions

General Journal

Date	Description	Post. Ref.	Debit	Credit

2 Ledger accounts opened

General Ledger

Station — Account No. 143

Date		Item	Post. Ref.	Debit	Credit	Balance Debit	Balance Credit

Accumulated Depreciation, Station — Account No. 144

Date		Item	Post. Ref.	Debit	Credit	Balance Debit	Balance Credit

3 Depreciation expense computed

Problem 14A-5 (continued)

4 Journal entry prepared for 1983 transaction

General Journal				
Date	Description	Post. Ref.	Debit	Credit

Name

Problem 14A-6

Purchase of Business with Goodwill Resulting

1 Journal entry prepared for Wright

General Journal				
Date	Description	Post. Ref.	Debit	Credit

2 Net assets exclusive of building computed

3 Goodwill computed

4 Journal entry prepared for Camp

General Journal

Date		Description	Post. Ref.	Debit	Credit

Name

Problem 5A-2
Preparation of Work Sheet, Adjusting Entries, and Closing Entries

1 Work sheet completed

James Laugh
Work
For the Year Ended

Account Name	Trial Balance Debit	Trial Balance Credit	Adjustme Debit
Cash	1375 -		
Accounts Receivable	2109 -		
Office Supplies	382 -		
Office Equipment	3755 -		
Accounts Payable		796 -	
Unearned Retainers		5000 -	
James Laughlin, Capital		4000 -	
James Laughlin, Withdrawals	6000 -		
Legal Fees		16200 -	
Rent Expense	1800 -		
Utility Expense	717 -		
Wages Expense	9858 -		
	25996 -	25996 -	

, Attorney

eet

ecember 31, 19xx

ts	Adjusted Trial Balance		Income Statement		Balance Sheet	
Credit	Debit	Credit	Debit	Credit	Debit	Credit

Name

Problem 5A-3
Completion of Work Sheet, Preparation of Financial Statements, Adjusting Entries, and Closing Entries

1 Work sheet completed

Drexel Th
Work Sh
For the Year Ended Se

Account Name	Trial Balance Debit	Trial Balance Credit	Adjustmen Debit
Cash	9800 -		
Accounts Receivable	8472 -		
Prepaid Insurance	9800 -		
Office Supplies	280 -		
Cleaning Supplies	1795 -		
Land	10000 -		
Building	200000 -		
Accumulated Depreciation, Building		18500 -	
Theater Furnishings	185000 -		
Accumulated Depreciation, Theater Furnishings		32500 -	
Office Equipment	15800 -		
Accumulated Depreciation, Office Equipment		7780 -	
Accounts Payable		22643 -	
Gift Books Liability		20950 -	
Mortgage Payable		150000 -	
Dave Parsons, Capital		156324 -	
Dave Parsons, Withdrawals	30000 -		
Ticket Sales		200000 -	
Theater Rental		22600 -	
Usher Wages Expense	92000 -		
Office Wages Expense	12000 -		
Utilities Expense	56350 -		
	631297 -	631297 -	

er

t

ember 30, 19xx

	Adjusted Trial Balance		Income Statement		Balance Sheet	
redit	Debit	Credit	Debit	Credit	Debit	Credit

· Repair Store

heet

ed May 31, 19xx

ts	Adjusted Trial Balance		Income Statement		Balance Sheet	
Credit	Debit	Credit	Debit	Credit	Debit	Credit

Name

Problem 5A-4 (continued)
The Complete Accounting Cycle—Two Months

3 May work sheet completed

Peterson Bicy
Work
For the Month E

Account Name	Trial Balance Debit	Trial Balance Credit	Adjustm Debit
Cash			
Prepaid Insurance			
Repair Supplies			
Repair Equipment			
Accounts Payable			
Mike Peterson, Capital			
Mike Peterson, Withdrawals			
Bicycle Repair Revenue			
Store Rent Expense			
Utility Expense			
Insurance Expense			
Repair Supplies Expense			
Depreciation Expense, Repair Equipment			
Accumulated Depreciation, Repair Equipment			
Net Income			

Name

Problem 5A-4 (continued)
The Complete Accounting Cycle—Two Months

8 June work sheet completed

Peterson Bicycle
Work Sh
For the Month Ende

Account Name	Trial Balance Debit	Trial Balance Credit	Adjustmen Debit
Cash			
Prepaid Insurance			
Repair Supplies			
Repair Equipment			
Accumulated Depreciation, Repair Equipment			
Accounts Payable			
Mike Peterson, Capital			
Mike Peterson, Withdrawals			
Bicycle Repair Revenue			
Store Rent Expense			
Utility Expense			
Insurance Expense			
Repair Supplies Expense			
Depreciation Expense, Repair Equipment			
Net Income			

epair Store

et

June 30, 19xx

	Adjusted Trial Balance		Income Statement		Balance Sheet	
redit	Debit	Credit	Debit	Credit	Debit	Credit

ling Lanes

heet

December 31, 19xx

ts	Adjusted Trial Balance		Income Statement		Balance Sheet	
Credit	Debit	Credit	Debit	Credit	Debit	Credit

Name

Problem 5A-5
Preparation of Work Sheet from Limited Data

1 Work sheet completed

Eastmoor Bov
Work S
For the Year Ended

Account Name	Trial Balance Debit	Trial Balance Credit	Adjustme Debit
Cash	12741 –		
Accounts Receivable	7388 –		
Supplies	1304 –		
Unexpired Insurance	1800 –		
Prepaid Advertising	900 –		
Land	5000 –		
Building	100000 –		
Accumulated Depreciation, Building		19000 –	
Equipment	125000 –		
Accumulated Depreciation, Equipment		22000 –	
Accounts Payable		14317 –	
Notes Payable		70000 –	
Unearned Revenue		2300 –	
Margaret Lord, Capital		60813 –	
Margaret Lord, Withdrawals	24000 –		
Revenue		614817 –	
Wages Expense	377114 –		
Advertising Expense	14300 –		
Utility Expense	42200 –		
Maintenance Expense	81300 –		
Miscellaneous Expense	10200 –		
	803247 –	803247 –	

Store

et

June 30, 19xx

	Income Statement		Balance Sheet	
:redit	Debit	Credit	Debit	Credit

Name

Problem 6A-2
Work Sheet, Income Statement, and Closing Entries for Merchandising Concern

1a Work sheet completed—adjusting entry method

Pepitone Boo
Work Sh
For the Period Ende

Account Name	Trial Balance Debit	Trial Balance Credit	Adjustments Debit
Cash	3175 -		
Accounts Receivable	9280 -		
Merchandise Inventory	29450 -		
Store Supplies	1911 -		
Prepaid Insurance	1600 -		
Store Equipment	37200 -		
Accumulated Depreciation, Store Equipment		14700 -	
Accounts Payable		12300 -	
Gary Pepitone, Capital		41994 -	
Gary Pepitone, Withdrawals	12000 -		
Sales		99400 -	
Sales Returns and Allowances	987 -		
Purchases	62300 -		
Purchases Returns and Allowances		1965 5 -	
Purchases Discounts		1356 -	
Freight In	2261 -		
Sales Salaries Expense	21350 -		
Rent Expense	3600 -		
Other Selling Expense	2614 -		
Utilities Expense	1677 -		
	189405 -	189405 -	

ok Store

heet

ed June 30, 19xx

nts	Income Statement		Balance Sheet	
Credit	Debit	Credit	Debit	Credit

Name

Problem 6A-2
Work Sheet, Income Statement, and Closing Entries for Merchandising Concern

1b Work sheet completed—closing entry method

Pepitone [cut off]
Work[cut off]
For the Period E[cut off]

Account Name	Trial Balance Debit	Trial Balance Credit	Adjustm[ents] Debit
Cash	3175 -		
Accounts Receivable	9280 -		
Merchandise Inventory	29450 -		
Store Supplies	1911 -		
Prepaid Insurance	1600 -		
Store Equipment	37200 -		
Accumulated Depreciation, Store Equipment		14700 -	
Accounts Payable		12300 -	
Gary Pepitone, Capital		41994 -	
Gary Pepitone, Withdrawals	12000 -		
Sales		99400 -	
Sales Returns and Allowances	987 -		
Purchases	62300 -		
Purchases Returns and Allowances		19655 -	
Purchases Discounts		1356 -	
Freight In	2261 -		
Sales Salaries Expense	21350 -		
Rent Expense	3600 -		
Other Selling Expense	2614 -		
Utilities Expense	1677 -		
	189405 -	189405 -	

	Income Statement		Balance Sheet	
redit	Debit	Credit	Debit	Credit

Name

Problem 6A-4
Work Sheet, Income Statement, and Closing Entries for Merchandising Concern

1a Work sheet prepared—adjusting entry method

McCandlish's Shoe Store
Work Sheet
For the Period Ended December 31, 19xx

Account Name	Trial Balance Debit	Trial Balance Credit	Adjustments Debit
Cash	2675 -		
Accounts Receivable	19307 -		
Merchandise Inventory	26500 -		
Store Supplies	951 -		
Prepaid Insurance	2600 -		
Store Equipment	32000 -		
Accumulated Depreciation, Store Equipment		19500 -	
Accounts Payable		22366 -	
Cheri McCandlish, Capital		63601 -	
Cheri McCandlish, Withdrawals	15000 -		
Sales		103000 -	
Sales Returns and Allowances	2150 -		
Purchases	61115 -		
Purchases Returns and Allowances		17310 -	
Purchases Discounts		1300 -	
Freight In	2144 -		
Rent Expense	4800 -		
Store Salaries Expense	41600 -		
Advertising Expense	14056 -		
Utility Expense	2179 -		
	227077 -	227077 -	

s Shoe Store

Sheet

December 31, 19xx

nts	Income Statement		Balance Sheet	
Credit	Debit	Credit	Debit	Credit

Name

Problem 6A-4
Work Sheet, Income Statement, and Closing Entries for Merchandising Concern

1b Work sheet prepared—closing entry method

McCandlish
Work
For the Period Ende

Account Name	Trial Balance Debit	Trial Balance Credit	Adjustm Debit
Cash	2675 -		
Accounts Receivable	19307 -		
Merchandise Inventory	26500 -		
Store Supplies	951 -		
Prepaid Insurance	2600 -		
Store Equipment	32000 -		
Accumulated Depreciation, Store Equipment		19500 -	
Accounts Payable		22366 -	
Cheri McCandlish, Capital		63601 -	
Cheri McCandlish, Withdrawals	15000 -		
Sales		103000 -	
Sales Returns and Allowances	2150 -		
Purchases	61115 -		
Purchases Returns and Allowances		17310 -	
Purchases Discounts		1300 -	
Freight In	2144 -		
Rent Expense	4800 -		
Store Salaries Expense	41600 -		
Advertising Expense	14056 -		
Utility Expense	2179 -		
	227077 -	227077 -	

ame

Problem 6A-5
Work Sheet, Income Statement, and Closing Entries for Merchandising Concern

a *Work sheet completed—adjusting entry method*

Barney's Camera

Work Shee

For the Year Ended Ju

Account Name	Trial Balance Debit	Trial Balance Credit	Adjustments Debit	Adjustments Cr
Cash	5857 -			
Accounts Receivable	34770 -			
Merchandise Inventory	176551 -			
Selling Supplies	826 -			
Office Supplies	1226 -			
Store Equipment	26400 -			
Accumulated Depreciation, Store Equipment		5600 -		
Office Equipment	9350 -			
Accumulated Depreciation, Office Equipment		3700 -		
Accounts Payable		56840 -		
Notes Payable		50000 -		
Barney Rand, Capital		155440 -		
Barney Rand, Withdrawals	18000 -			
Sales		396457 -		
Sales Returns and Allowances	11250 -			
Purchases	218350 -			
Purchases Returns and Allowances		26450 -		
Purchases Discounts		3788 -		
Freight In	10078 -			
Store Salaries Expense	106500 -			
Office Salaries Expense	26400 -			
Advertising Expense	18200 -			
Rent Expense	14400 -			
Insurance Expense	2800 -			
Utility Expense	17317 -			
	698275 -	698275 -		

Store

ne 30, 19xx

	Income Statement		Balance Sheet	
edit	Debit	Credit	Debit	Credit

mera Store					
Sheet					
d June 30, 19xx					
nts	Income Statement		Balance Sheet		
Credit	Debit	Credit	Debit	Credit	

Name

Problem 6A-5
Work Sheet, Income Statement, and Closing Entries for Merchandising Concern

1b Work sheet completed—closing entry method

Barney's C
Work
For the Year En

Account Name	Trial Balance Debit	Trial Balance Credit	Adjustm Debit
Cash	5857 -		
Accounts Receivable	34770 -		
Merchandise Inventory	176551 -		
Selling Supplies	826 -		
Office Supplies	1226 -		
Store Equipment	26400 -		
Accumulated Depreciation, Store Equipment		5600 -	
Office Equipment	9350 -		
Accumulated Depreciation, Office Equipment		3700 -	
Accounts Payable		56840 -	
Notes Payable		50000 -	
Barney Rand, Capital		155440 -	
Barney Rand, Withdrawals	18000 -		
Sales		396457 -	
Sales Returns and Allowances	11250 -		
Purchases	218350 -		
Purchases Returns and Allowances		26450 -	
Purchases Discounts		3788 -	
Freight In	10078 -		
Store Salaries Expense	106500 -		
Office Salaries Expense	26400 -		
Advertising Expense	18200 -		
Rent Expense	14400 -		
Insurance Expense	2800 -		
Utility Expense	17317 -		
	698275 -	698275 -	

ster

Office Supplies Debit	Sales Salaries Debit	Office Salaries Debit	Selling Maint. Debit	Office Maint. Debit	Utilities Debit	Other Accounts	
						Name	Debit

ne

Problem 8A-5
Voucher System Transactions

Voucher register, check register, and journal entries prepared and transactions recorded

Voucher Reg

Date	Vou. No.	Payee	Payment Date	Payment Check No.	Vouchers Payable Credit	Purchases Debit	Freight In Debit	Store Suppli Debi

Register

ore plies bit	Office Supplies Debit	Sales Salaries Debit	Office Salaries Debit	Selling Maint. Debit	Office Maint. Debit	Utilities Debit	Other Accounts Name	 Debit

Name

Problem 8A-6
Voucher System Transactions

1 Voucher register, check register, and journal entries prepared and transactions recorded

Voucher								
			Payment		Vouchers		Freight	
	Vou.			Check	Payable	Purchases	In	Su
Date	No.	Payee	Date	No.	Credit	Debit	Debit	

Register

Deductions				Distribution	
FICA Tax	Federal Income Tax	Supplemental Benefits Plan	Payment	Sales Expense	Administrative Expense
	40 50				
	20 75				
	412 50				
	35 60				
	60 50				
	23 00				
	241 00				
	30 00				

Name

Problem 12A-6
Payroll Register and Related Entries

Payroll register prepared

Payrol

Pay Period: October 31

Employee	Total Hours	Earnings: Regular	Earnings: Overtime	Earnings: Gross	Earnings: Cumulative
Austin, L.					
Cox, C.					
Glasskins, I.					
Lzak, L.					
Recknor, P.					
Sloan, S.					
Tokoly, Q.					
Yee, B.